LEVEL **2B**

PIANO
Adventures®

Arranged by Nancy and Randall Faber

THE BASIC PIANO METHOD

CONTENTS

Don't Cry for Me, Argentina

Key of _____ Major

Words by
Tim Rice

Music by
Andrew Lloyd Webber

Teacher Duet: (Student plays 1 octave higher, without pedal)

*Teacher Note: Circled finger numbers (indicating hand position changes) have been included as a reading aid.
For the remainder of this book, circled numbers are omitted when a musical passage is repeated.

FF1?

DISCOVERY How is the music different when the opening melody returns at *measure 17*?

The 3 C's of Sightreading

The word *sightreading* means to play music without earlier practice.

- Sightread the five musical examples that follow. Each example uses a **rhythm** from *Don't Cry for Me, Argentina*; however, some notes have been changed.

The following **3 C's** will help you with sightreading.

 CORRECT HAND POSITION
Find the correct starting note for each hand.

 COUNT - OFF
Set a steady tempo by counting one "free" measure before starting to play.

 CONCENTRATE
Focus your eyes on the music, carefully reading the intervals.

1.
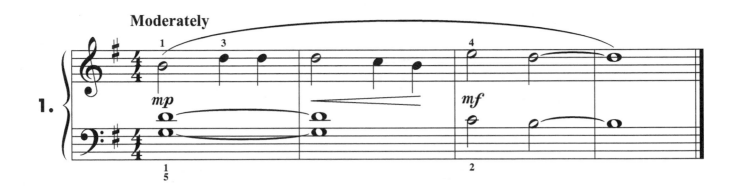

2.
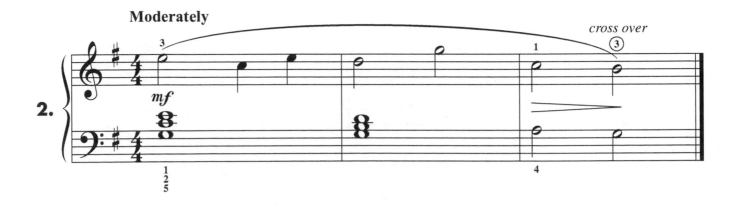

DON'T CRY FOR ME, ✻ARGENTINA✻

3.

4.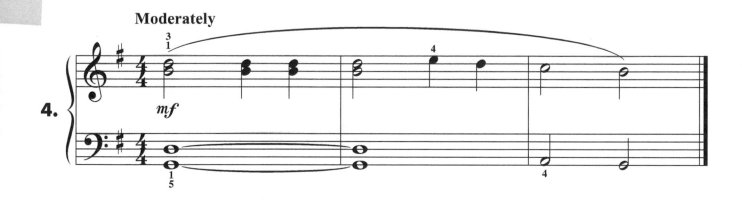

5.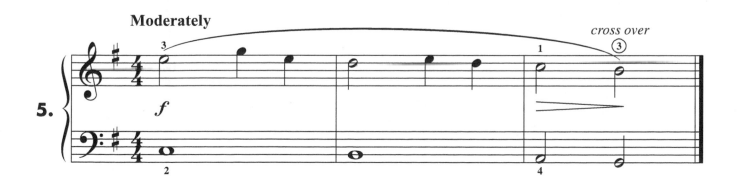

I Want to Hold Your Hand

Key of _____ Major

Moderately fast

By John Lennon and Paul McCartney

DISCOVERY Point out two measures where the L.H. plays *only* **half steps**.

FF12

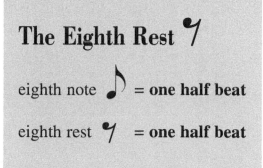

The Eighth Rest

eighth note ♪ = one half beat

eighth rest ♪ = one half beat

I Want to Hold Your Hand

By John Lennon and Paul McCartney

- Write "**1 and 2 and 3 and 4 and**" (abbreviated **1 + 2 + 3 + 4 +**) below the notes for each of these rhythms. Notice that each beat is divided into two equal parts.

- Then play, counting aloud.

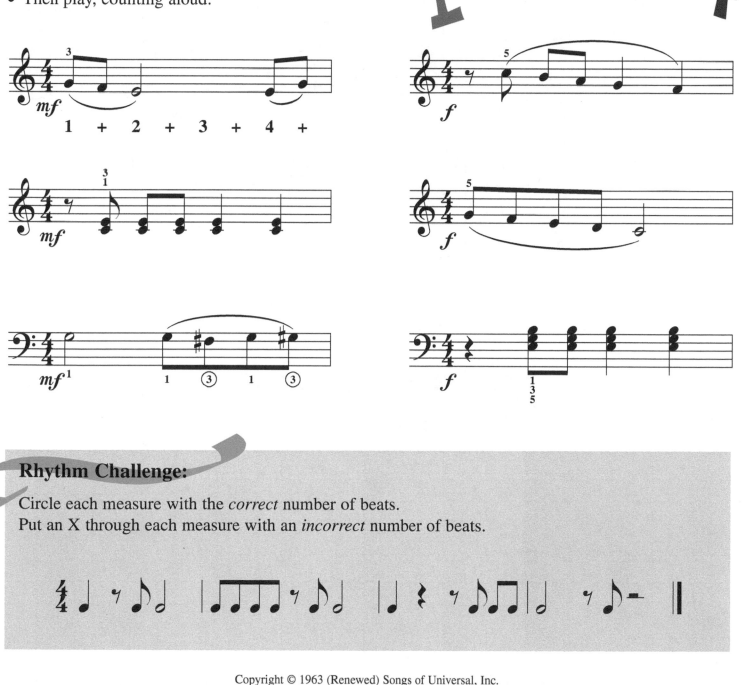

Rhythm Challenge:

Circle each measure with the *correct* number of beats.
Put an X through each measure with an *incorrect* number of beats.

Linus and Lucy
from the *PEANUTS* Television Specials

Key of _____ Major

By Vince Guaraldi

Brightly

(prepare L.H.)

Teacher Duet: (Student plays 1 octave higher)

FF1

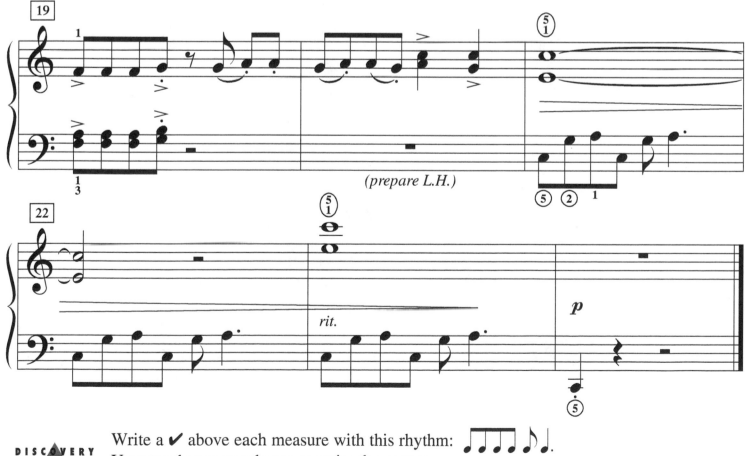

DISCOVERY

Write a ✔ above each measure with this rhythm: ♪♪♪♪ ♪♪ ♩.
Your teacher may ask you to write the counts
1 + 2 + 3 + 4 + in *measure 1*. (Write in the middle of the grand staff.)

THEORY ACTIVITY

. . . Music Theory for Linus and Lucy

The Doctor is in

? for Linus

Name the **intervals** in the boxes (2nd, 3rd, 4th, 5th, 6th).

? for Lucy

Write the counts **1 + 2 + 3 + 4 +** under the notes.

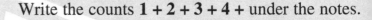

? for Linus

Draw a *diminuendo* sign below.
What does it mean?

sign:

meaning:

? for Lucy

Name both notes.
Then draw this **6th** one octave *higher*.

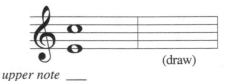
(draw)

upper note ___

lower note ___

10

? for Linus

For the musical example shown below:

Circle the count where each **accent** (>) occurs.

1 + 2 + 3 + 4 +

Circle the count where the *staccato* occurs.

1 + 2 + 3 + 4 +

? for Lucy

Draw a **flat** (♭) *to the left* of each note.
Name both notes. Then name the **interval**.

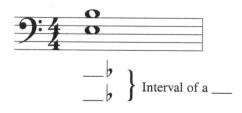

—♭
—♭ } Interval of a ___

? for Linus

What is the abbreviation for *ritardando*?
What does it mean?

abbreviation:

meaning:

? for Lucy

Draw a line to connect each rest on
the staff to its correct name below.

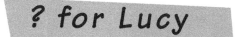

whole rest   half rest   quarter rest   eighth rest

? for Linus

Draw four *different* **C's** on the grand staff below.

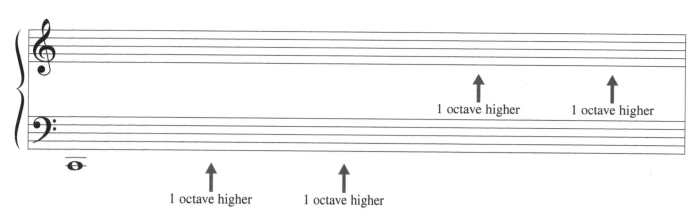

1 octave higher   1 octave higher

1 octave higher   1 octave higher

The River

Key of _____ Major

Words and Music by
Victoria Shaw and Garth Brooks

Moderately fast ("in two")

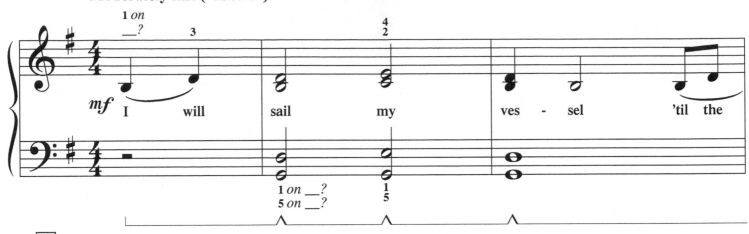

I will sail my ves - sel 'til the riv - er runs dry. _____ Like a

Teacher Duet: (Student plays 2 octaves higher, without pedal)

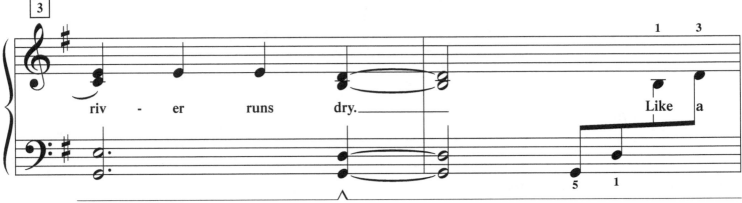

FF1

bird on the wind, _____ these wa - ters are my

sky. I'll nev - er reach my des - ti - na - tion

if I nev - er try. So I will sail my

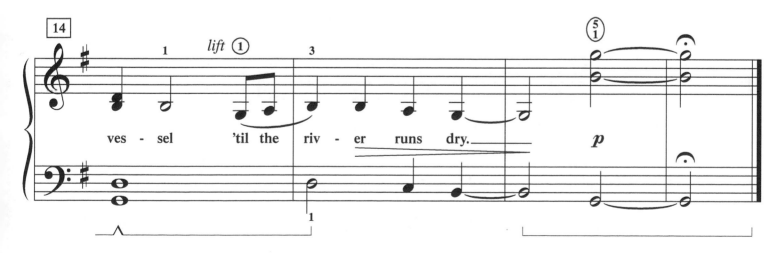

ves - sel 'til the riv - er runs dry. _____

DISCOVERY Point out a *crescendo* and *diminuendo* in this piece.
What do these musical terms mean?

The River of Chords

In popular music, the "lead" (pronounced LEED) means the melody.
A lead sheet is the *melody only*, with **chord symbols** written above.

Note: Chord letter names are written *above* the staff.
Roman numerals are written *below* the staff.

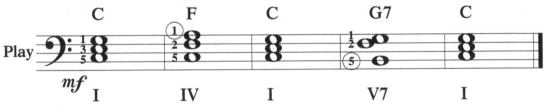

Practice Suggestions:

- First play the melody alone.

- Then *harmonize* the melody with your left hand.
Play **blocked I, IV,** and **V7 chords** as indicated
by the chord symbols.

The River
Lead Sheet

Key of C

Words and Music by
Victoria Shaw and Garth Brooks

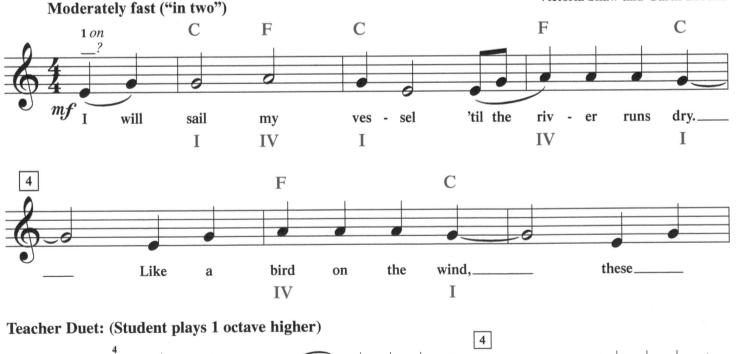

Moderately fast ("in two")

I will sail my ves - sel 'til the riv - er runs dry.

Like a bird on the wind, these

Teacher Duet: (Student plays 1 octave higher)

FF1?

wa - ters   are   my   sky.   I'll   nev - er   reach   my   des - ti -

IV   V7   I   IV

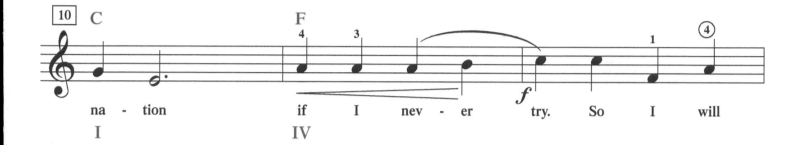

na - tion   if   I   nev - er   try.   So   I   will

I   IV

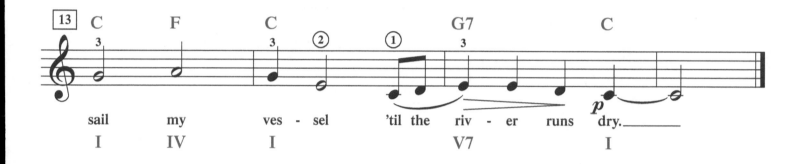

sail   my   ves - sel   'til the   riv - er   runs   dry._____

I   IV   I   V7   I

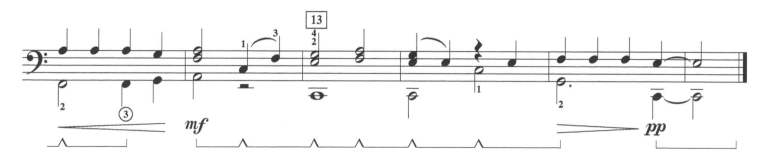

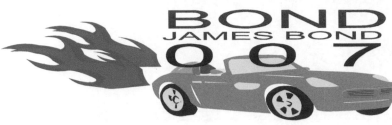

The James Bond Theme

Key of A minor

Music by
Monty Norman

Moderately fast

FF1

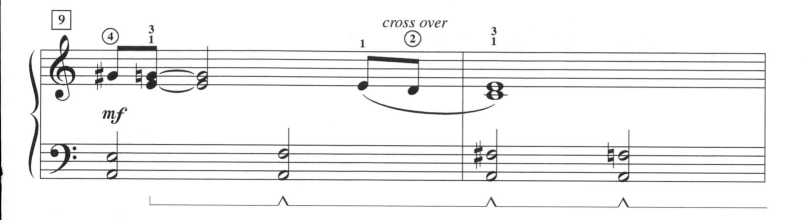

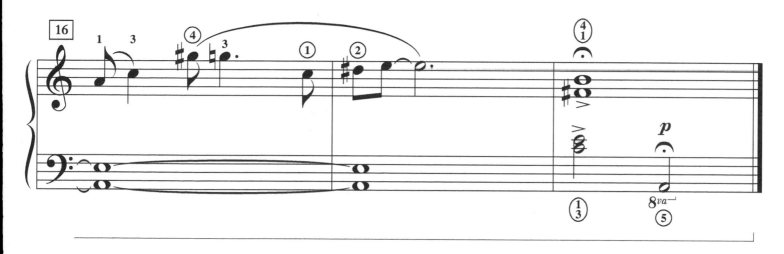

DISCOVERY

How is the music different when the opening measures return at *measure 11*?

A Key Investigation

These examples from *The James Bond Theme* have gone "undercover" to different minor keys.

Play each example on the piano and name the minor key in the magnifying glass.

The James Bond Theme

Music by
Monty Norman

FF1

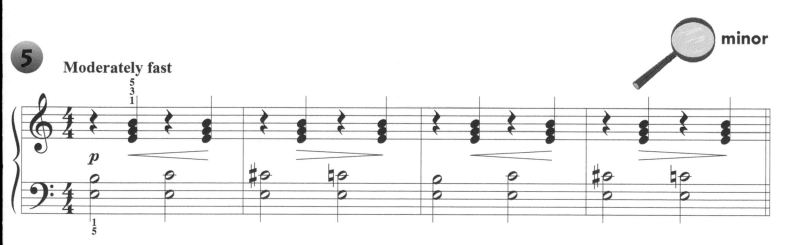

259

Ashokan Farewell

Key of _____ Major

By
Jay Ungar

Gently flowing

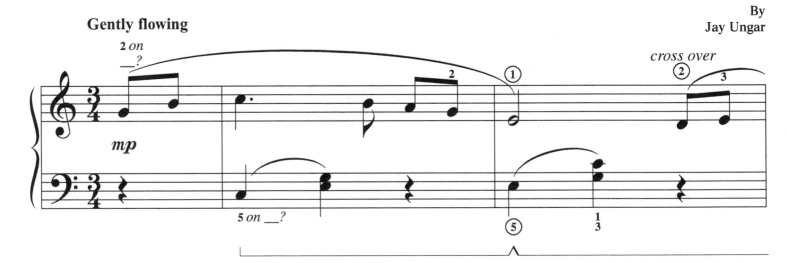

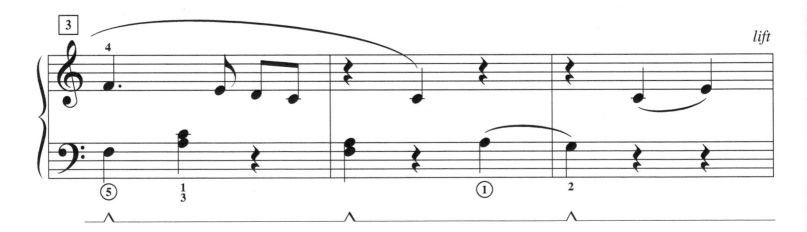

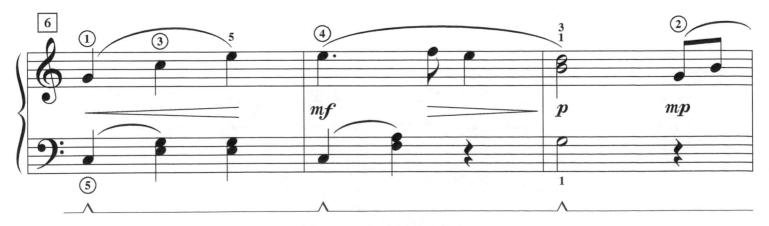

FF1?

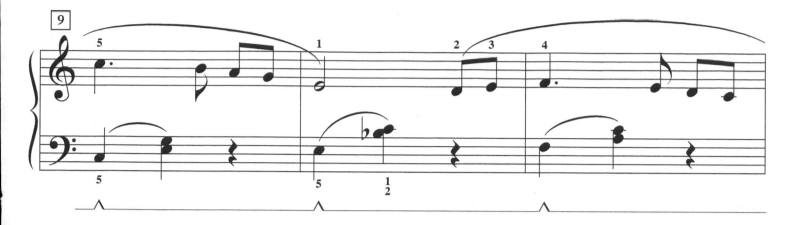

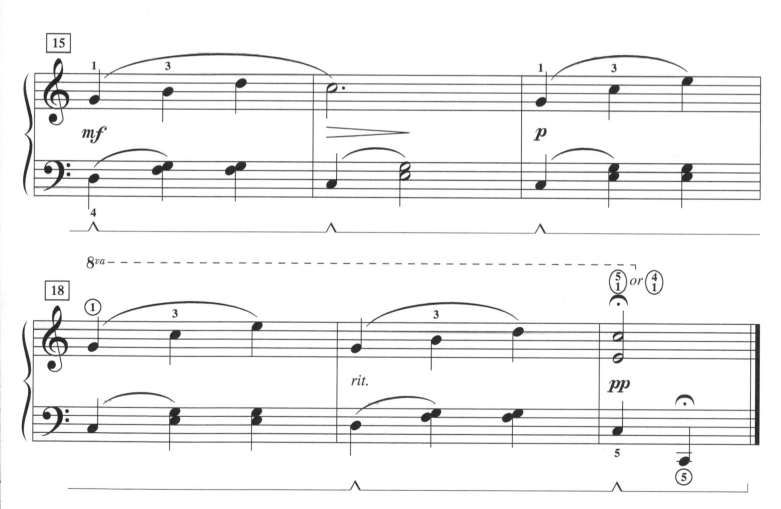

DISCOVERY Put a ✔ above eight measures that use
only notes of the C chord (C - E - G).

Ashokan Duet

A pianist reads from a musical score when playing with another instrument(s). The score shows the solo instrument on top (with smaller notes) and the piano part below on the grand staff.

The instrument solo for *Ashokan Farewell* may be played on the flute, a digital keyboard (setting of your choice), or simply the piano.

Practice Suggestions:

- First write **I**, **IV**, or **V7** in the box below each measure.

- Learn your part thoroughly before playing the duet. Observe all dynamics!

Ashokan Farewell

By
Jay Ungar

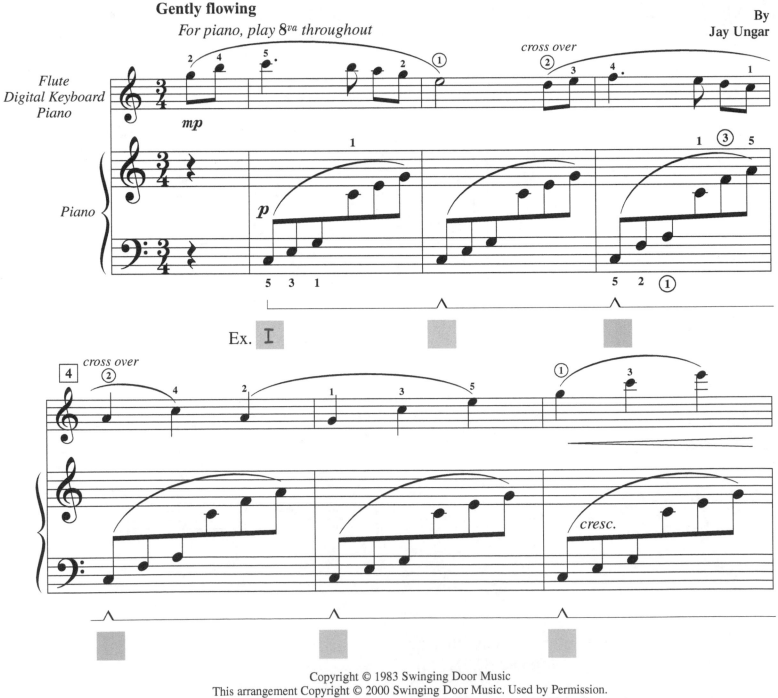

FF1

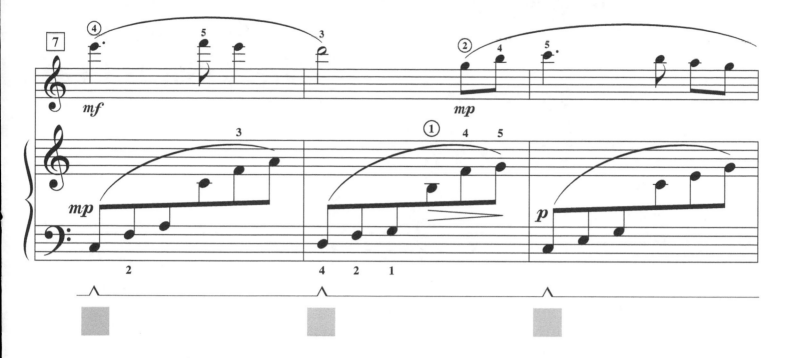

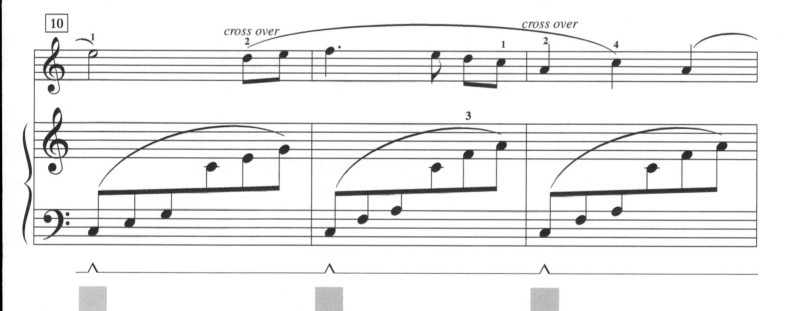

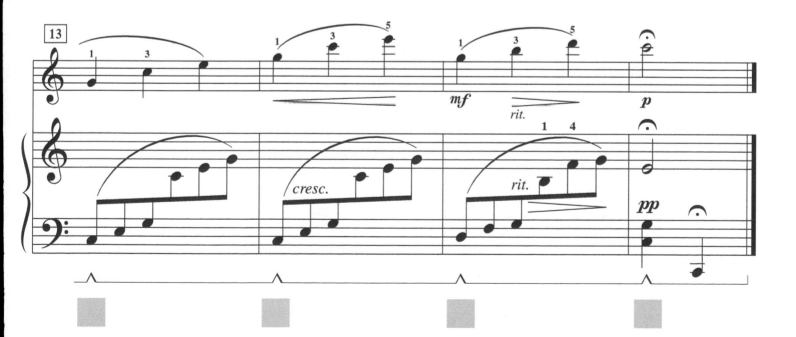

Ding-Dong!
The Witch Is Dead
from THE WIZARD OF OZ

Lyric by
E.Y. Harburg

Music by
Harold Arlen

Key of _____ Major

FF1?

gone where the gob - lins go be - low, be - low, be - low, yo -

ho. Let's o - pen up and sing and ring the bells out.

cross over

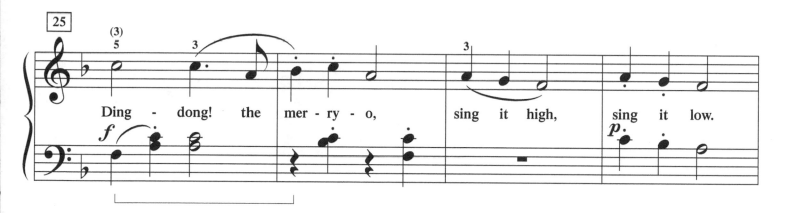

Ding - dong! the mer - ry - o, sing it high, sing it low.

Let them know the wick - ed witch is dead!

DISCOVERY An **accidental** is a sharp, flat, or natural that is not in the key signature.
Circle all the accidentals in this piece. (Hint: There are 4.)

"... Sing it high, Sing it low"

Your teacher will play example **a** or **b**.
- Watch the notes and *listen* carefully to the **rhythm**.
- Then circle the "bell" for each example you hear.

(Teacher Note: The examples may be played several times.)

Ding-Dong!
The Witch Is Dead

Music by
Harold Arlen

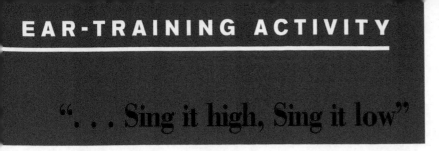

Ring the bells out!

Which old witch?

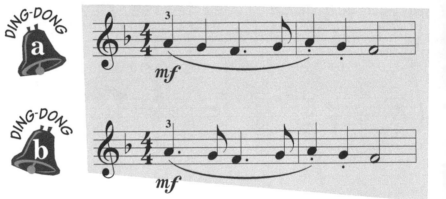

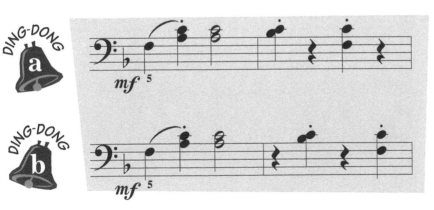

Ding-Dong!

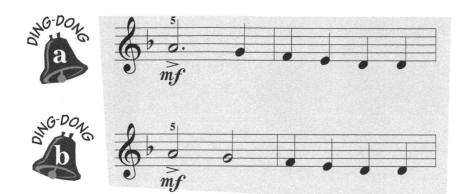

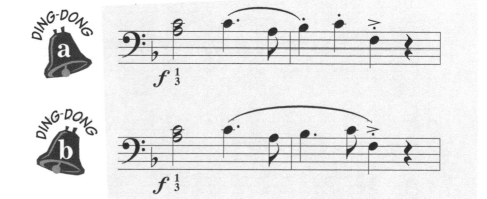

Rhythm Challenge: Your teacher may ask you to clap
(or tap) the rhythm for each example.

dreams really do come true!

Over the Rainbow
from *THE WIZARD OF OZ*

Key of _____ Major

Lyric by
E.Y. Harburg

Music by
Harold Arlen

Flowing gently

Some - where o - ver the rain - bow

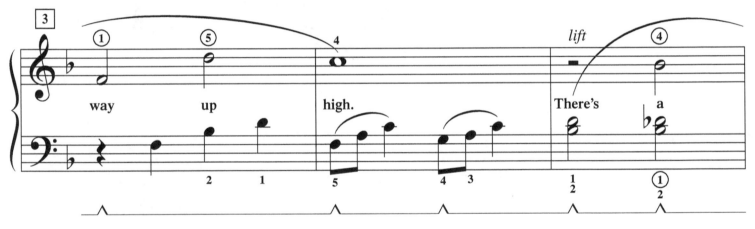

way up high. There's a

Teacher Duet: (Student plays 1 octave higher, without pedal)

FF1

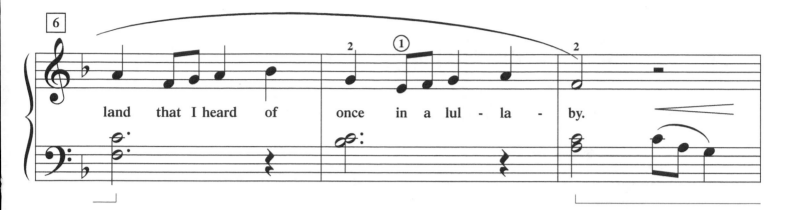

land   that I heard   of   once   in a lul - la - by.

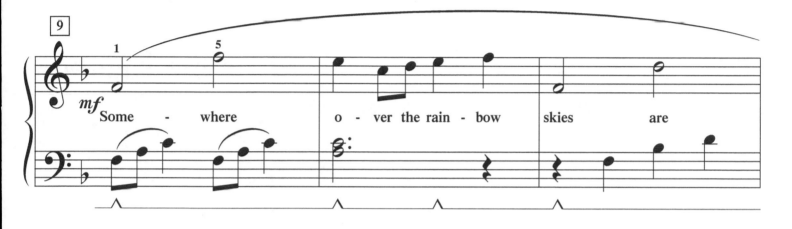

mf Some - where   o - ver the rain - bow   skies   are

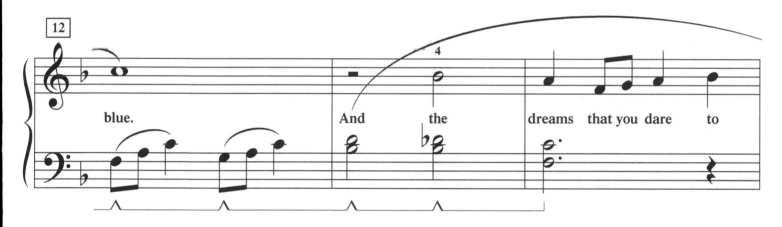

blue.   And   the   dreams   that you dare   to

dream   real - ly do   come   true.   *rit.*

L.H. ②/④ *over*

A *descending* F major scale (F E D C B♭ A G F) is "hidden" in the melody of
Over the Rainbow. Find and circle these notes as they appear in the R.H. melody.

Rainbow Scale Steps

The notes of a scale are called *scale steps*. Each scale step has a number.

F Major scale steps

scale steps 1   2   3   4   5   6   7   8 (1)

1a. First name each note in the box given.

b. Then write the number of the **scale step** in the blank below.

Over the Rainbow

Music by
Harold Arlen

Lyrics by
E.Y. Harburg

FF1

2. In each pot of gold, name the *intervals* found in the opening melody of *Over the Rainbow*—**2nd**, **3rd**, **4th**, **5th**, **6th**, or **octave (8ve)**.

Over the Rainbow in F Major

Intervals: **Ex.** 8ve

mf Some - where   o - ver the rain - bow   way   up   high.

Transposition: To play music in a different key.

When transposing, the note names change, but the *intervals* stay the same. Reading the intervals and listening to the sound will help you transpose.

---

3. Now transpose the opening melody to the **Key of G Major** (up a whole step).

Look at the intervals in F major and *listen to the sound* to help you transpose.

Over the Rainbow in G Major

Rhythm:

mf Some - where   o - ver the rain - bow   way   up   high.

---

4. Now transpose the opening measures of *Over the Rainbow* to the **Key of C Major.**

Over the Rainbow in C Major

Rhythm:

mf Some - where   o - ver the rain - bow   way   up   high.

---

5. Play each of these examples in the Keys of F major, G major, and C major. You may enjoy singing the melody. Which key do you prefer?

MUSIC DICTIONARY

pp	*p*	*mp*	*mf*	*f*	*ff*
pianissimo	*piano*	*mezzo piano*	*mezzo forte*	*forte*	*fortissimo*
very soft	soft	medium soft	medium loud	loud	very loud

crescendo (cresc.)
Play gradually louder.

diminuendo (dim.) or decrescendo (decresc.)
Play gradually softer.

SIGN	TERM	DEFINITION
	accent mark	Play this note louder.
	accidental	A sharp or flat that is not in the key signature. A natural is also an accidental.
	accompaniment	The harmony and rhythm that accompany the melody.
	blocked chord	The notes of a chord played together.
	broken chord	The notes of a chord played separately.
	chord	Three or more notes sounding together.
	I ("one") chord	Three notes built up in 3rds from the tonic note.
	IV ("four") chord	Three notes built up in 3rds from the fourth note of the scale.
	V7 ("five-seven")	A four-note chord built up in 3rds from the dominant note (step 5 of the scale), often played with only two or three notes.
	damper pedal	The pedal on the right. It lifts the dampers off the strings, allowing the sound to continue to ring.
	**dominant**	The fifth note of the scale.
	dotted quarter note	A dot adds half the value to the note. A dotted quarter note equals a quarter note tied to an eighth note.
	duet	A musical piece for two instruments or voices.
	dynamics	The "louds and softs" of music. See dynamic marks above.
	eighth rest	Silence for the value of an eighth note.
	fermata	Hold this note longer than its usual value.
	fifth (5th)	The interval of a 5th spans five letter names. (Ex. C up to G, or A down to D) Line-(skip-a-line)-line, or space-(skip-a-space)-space.
	1st and 2nd endings	Play the 1st ending and take the repeat. Then play the 2nd ending, skipping over the 1st ending.
	flat	A flat lowers a note one half step.
	fourth (4th)	The interval of a 4th spans four letter names. (Ex. C up to F, or A down to E) Line-(skip-a-line)-space. or space-(skip-a-space)-line.
	half rest	Silence for two counts or beats.
	half step	The distance from one key to the very closest key on the keyboard. (Ex. C-C♯ or E-F)
	harmony	Notes or chords that accompany a melody.
	imitation	The immediate repetition of a musical idea in another voice.
	interval	The distance between two musical tones or keys on the keyboard. For example, 2nd, 3rd, 4th, 5th, octave.